Wording the Land

Poetry Collection 2019

Jefferson County Farmers Markets

Publishing Partners

finnriver farm
eggs
laid in chimacum

EGGS $5
DUCK $6

Publishing Partners
Port Townsend, WA 98368
www.marciabreece.com

Copyright © 2019 Jefferson County Farmers Markets

All rights reserved. No part of this book may be reproduced, stored in, or introduced into a retrieval system, or transmitted in any form, or by any means (electronic, mechanical, photocopying, recording, or otherwise) without the prior written permission of the Jefferson Country Farmers Markets Organization.

Jefferson County Farmers Markets
PO Box 1384
Port Townsend, WA 98368
info@jcfmarkets.org

Printed in USA

Illustrations: Amanda Milholland
Photo page 69: Crystie Kisler
Photo page 38: Jen Lee
Other photos: Marcia Breece

To order copies of this book, email:
wordingtheland@gmail.com

ISBN: 978-1-944887-51-3

Poems and Poets

Gratitude vii
Wording the Land Project.. viii
Holly's Farm | Frank Handler 1
Can You? | Sym Sebastian 2
Autumnal Equinox | David Shiah 3
Along I-5, Yuba County | Nancy Fowler 4
Mutton | Liz Crain 6
Fox On The Run | Liz Crain 7
Nature Never Hurries | David Shiah 9
Untitled | Doug Milholland 10
Eutopos Huckleberry Harvest | Karen A. Grooms 11
At Sunset, June Horizon | Sheila Bender 13
Work Around | Sheila Bender 14
Every Day Excitement | Sheila Bender 15
Ode To Raspberries | Hazel Windstorm 16
Chimacum Valley Suite | Holly J. Hughes 18
Farm Tour The Day Before Equinox | Holly J. Hughes 20
The Woman In The Garden | Heather Hamilton 22
In The Orchard | Irene Bloom 24
Untitled | Christine Walsh Rogers 26
wonderwoman | afrose fatima ahmed 28
an ode to wednesday market | afrose fatima ahmed 29
an ode to the saturday market | afrose fatima ahmed 30
Another Ode To Autumn | Carol Light 31
Wording The Land Guest Poets 32
Lunch With the Devil | Matthew Nienow 34
Allergy Song | Matthew Nienow 36
Spring Planting | Matthew Nienow 37

Finnriver Pantoum | Roseanna Almaee-Nejadi 39
Wording the Land | Roseanna Almaee-Nejadi.............................. 40
Untitled | Roxane Hudson 41
Untitled | Diane Morency.. 42
Hooray, Hooray, It's Market Day | Judy Drechsler...................... 44
Farm Tour Perfume | Lynn Fritsche 46
Five Hiaku | Oma Landstra 47
Spring Equinox | Sheila Bender for Judith Kitchen 48
Untitled | Pierce Kennedy.. 49
Bzzzzzz | Richard Coletta.. 50
Walk Straight | Kia Armstrong... 52
Feeding he Goats At Sunfield | Alex C. Eisenberg 53
Fall Fog Has Settled Again Over Discovery Bay | Sheila Bender................ 55
Curves and Angles | Leticia Huber 57
Brightness | Liz Crain 61
St. Helens | Peter G. Quinn.. 62
Chimacum Jr. Sr. High School Garden | Margaret Garrett 63
A Farmer's Poem | Halcyon Stoker-Graham 64
Seasons in the Orchard | Crystie Kisler 66
Winter Wheat | Abby Jorgensen 68
Muffin Therapy | Irene Bloom.. 70
Souvlaki | Irene Bloom 72
In Ghent | Irene Bloom 73
About the Publisher 74

Gratitude

Hearty thanks to poets Gary Lilley, Afrose Fatima Ahmed, Carol Light and Matthew Nienow for offering generous support for this project in the form of readings, workshops, and poems.

Thanks to Kat Mullins for her enthusiasm and assistance and to poet-farmer Sam Robison for helping coordinate the project and publishing!

With gratitude to Marcia Breece for the generous donation of her time and talent to layout and publish this volume for us! Learn more about her work on page seventy-four.

Wording the Land Project

Wording the Land began as a small seed of an idea between several farmers and creators centered in the Chimacum Valley. Instinctively, we knew there was a meaningful connection between the desire to create—to write, to paint, to express one's inner life—and the work we each performed in the soil, fields, woods and streams. A brief bout of research yielded historical precedent. There is an ancient etymological connection between the root word of the verb 'create' and the goddess Ceres, the Roman goddess of cultivation and grains. The word 'create' comes to us from the early fifteenth century, from the Latin creatus, past participle of creare, "to make, bring forth, produce, procreate, beget, cause," and directly relates to Ceres and to crescere, "arise, be born, increase, grow."

The Wording the Land project proceeded with a sincere desire to bring poets and writers to the farms surrounding this community, and to find those already there. Over the course of Farm Tour's 2019 weekend, we invited visitors to farms to take a moment and consider their own relationship to the land, the food it produces, and the people who work its soil.

We also solicited writers throughout the Fall—at the local Farmers Markets and through general outreach—to contribute poems. With the help of four distinguished poets—Afrose Fatima Ahmed, Gary Lilley, Carol Light and Matt Nienow—whose work is featured within, we held a series of workshops and readings along this theme. From community contributors of all ages and poetic experience, we have compiled this small and precious journal.

As you read through the poems inspired by the land and food-creating community here, we hope you'll come to celebrate the unique and vital marriage of art and farming in Jefferson County. And we want to thank you for purchasing a book that not only supports local artists and farmers, but local food access efforts as well. Proceeds raised from the sale of this collection will be contributed to Jefferson County Farmers Markets food access programs, which provide matching funds for shoppers when they use SNAP and other federal food assistance dollars at the farmers markets.

Lastly, we want to thank our generous sponsors and devoted partners. This book would not be possible without funding from The Port Townsend Arts Commission, and support from Finnriver Farm & Cidery, Jefferson Countory Farmers Markets, and land and food-loving citizens like you.

For inquires or more ways to get involved in the future, please email: wordingtheland@gmail.com.

Holly's Farm

Frank Handler

Is a poem ever done

Old words pulled
New ones planted
Let them germinate, take root

Pruning
To bear the weight of meaning

The thought remains
The same
Just to express it better

Each word, each row
A pathway to the next

Control, Alt, Till

Can You?

Sym Sebastian

Can you put your ear to the ground and hear the worms doing the wiggle dance?
Can you feel the dirty fingernails from natures manicure?
Can you smell the fresh, invisible, irreplaceable air?
Can you see the yellow leaf in a tight spin, effortlessly guided by its partner the wind?
Can you taste the farm to fork bounty?

Autumnal Equinox

David Shiah

Summer warmth yields to on-coming autumn
Slower days and softer nights beckon
Life giving rains nourish the thirsty earth as
the land rests now; quiet, tranquil.
Nature slows, readying for winter depths
Forest gnomes gleefully gather mushrooms while
falling leaves go out in a blaze of splendor.
Mighty Orion commands the mystical night sky
Season of inner contemplation, reflection
Welcome autumn, what magic will you bring?

Along I-5, Yuba County

Nancy Fowler

Breakthrough sun
scatters against stainless steel,
grain silos, hovering sentinels,
above furrowed rows of hopeful seedlings,
a promise of harvest's fulfillment;
across the field, a shadowy border
of ordered trees-dormant almonds-
each holds its breeze-washed limbs exultant,
like ballerinas in attitude en pointe.

Ten and fifty trumpeter swans
drift on the mirror glaze
of still sleeping rice paddies,
graceful heads dabbling for submerged tubers
and emergent grasses; one by one, great egrets rise
    languorously from flood-swollen fields,
sated with spring's generosity of fingerlings and
    mouse pups. From phone poles and cattails,
male red-winged blackbirds, feathers fluffed,
trill their mating song
to females foraging in fresh grass
that hugs the asphalt roadside.

Laughter punctuates the squish and release of
now mud-filled shoes.
We plunge into lushness, slurping
through fecund earth, to gather
armloads of tangy mustard, and crunchable
miners lettuce, with signature white-blue stars
that fleck the fleece against which
they are embraced, and, like all gatherers,
we nibble now and then from our harvest
to ingest the season's bounty.
Mustard glow dazzles this drizzly day.

Mutton

Liz Crain

In still firelight gazing under starry night
Your soft grace chanced upon a moonbeam
Angels sang a wanton song of absolute acceptance
When this elaborate praise comes hither
Be ready to catch such flattery on the wind
In old skin writhing like worm on hook,
The stench of rot resounding
When time has taken all she's worth
We'll see you in the morning
Laid out in mortem's firm embrace
Love's last heart song disgraced
For in you there is onion, sage
And round you we say grace.

Fox On The Run

Liz Crain

As the sun sets west there is one scent on the air
Another four-legged thief takes the last duck
In quiet dusk there is no sound of struggle
Another of Mother Nature's sons has done the deed
When can we take our revenge upon a thief?
How does one life beg the other in this twist
    of fate?
For the sake of forgiveness, there must be
    no remorse,
But a second try will find the fox hung on a nail by
    the barn
No understanding for a grievance of this kind
Take from those who have taken, life for a life
In the end, there is no judge, jury, or sentence
Steady hands cocked trigger, hold steady for
    the pull

Nature Never Hurries

David Shiah

Soft, green fern slowly unravels
Newborn fawn gazes in wonder
While the old-growth forest slumbers
Moss and mushrooms content
Moist, warm earth, full of life
Finnriver lands flourish under the summer sun
As a gentle zephyr caresses the flowered meadow
Nature never hurries, yet everything gets done

Untitled

Doug Milholland

When we cook, when we sit to eat
    Gratitude comes through us
In our pausing reflection we give thanks
    to your hands grew our food
    tended four-legged ones that give us
    milk, cheese, meat
        as we reflect on our living world
    tended by our gardeners, working,
        dawn to dusk
        so steady and so strong
        tending the work that must be done.

Eutopos Huckleberry Harvest

Karen A. Grooms

Washed by the rain
      Warmed by the sun

Loved on by Nature's bees
                      hummingbirds
                              butterflies

Plumped through Summertime
      Cooled from the breeze

Each century grown stem
        visited through the season
             three, four, maybe five times

Every tiny ripe orb
        released by a gentle hand
          sorted with care

Just for this moment.

This bursting juicy sweet tart moment
      flooding our senses
          with black purple goodness.

At Sunset, June Horizon

Sheila Bender

Cedar and fir trees at the edge of the bay
are an audience in front row seats. They wear
shawls, have colicky hair. But I can see
between them to the orange band in the sky,
bright against the grey blue bay and a coming
cloud cover. From the cheap seats in the back,
I gaze over the heads of salal bushes, of Oregon
Grape. Evening arrives to the songs of birds,
the soft croaking of frogs. Here is an orchestra
for the sky's choreography. I watch. I eat a late
dinner. I savor the sweetness of blueberries
still warm from a day's bright sun.

Work Around

Sheila Bender

After Viewing Denise Champion's Oil "Storm Coming"

There may always be a storm coming,
but there are not always storms.

There may not always be a far horizon,
but there is always something we can reach for.

Fields may not always be green,
but there are always seeds in the fallow.

Every Day Excitement

Sheila Bender

While the sales woman snips the nylon thread
    that secures
the little plastic bag that holds an extra button
    for the newly
purchased shirt I plan on wearing right from
    the store,
I think
    button up,
        buttonholes,
            boutonnieres,
                circles of sliced
                    shallots tonight
                        popping in the frying pan.

Ode To Raspberries

Hazel Windstorm

Polished brown stalks shine in the evening sun
Delicate thorns bristle from the mahogany wood
The harsh winter wind rattles the leafless stalks
Yellow grass weaves itself around their roots
They curve gracefully toward the grey skies
The occasional bare stem peeks from between
    their thorns

Tiny leaves uncurl neatly outward
Pure shafts of sunlight soak into the leaves
The once brown stalks suffused with a soft green
    mist of leaves
Bunches of leaves erupt from the earth
Early bees hurriedly zoom across the modest
    white flowers
Runners burst forth from the dirt, persistent
    as thistles

Clusters of berries adorn the bushy branches
Tiny emerald tree frogs nestle in the nursery
    of leaves
Birds float down to feast on the delicate fruit
The ruffled plants saturated in summer sunlight
Bees, drowsed with warmth, hum lazily across
    the dandelions
The plants explode across the paths, berries
    brushing the ground

Sun dances across the many tiny orbs crafted together
They are not solitary fruits, clustering, instead, in brilliant bunches
The bright white cores remain on their stems, even after the berry is plucked
An explosion of scarlet against the emerald background
Leaf fringed stalks brushed with berries
The once brown landscape now a riot of green

Leftover berries hang sadly from their stems
They disintegrate into sweet puddles on the ground
Sticky, discolored, fruit adhered to the rotting cores
Yellow-jackets crawl, drunk on sweetness
Leaves shrivel and collect into drifts on the dirt
The once bold stalks are bare again

Chimacum Valley Suite

Holly J. Hughes

I. Walking, Dawn

This morning, fog hangs
in the valley as cows low
to each other, adrift
in the fields like whales
echolocating, ships navigating
the fog banks. *I'm here,* one calls.
we are too, we answer.

II. Compost

Earth, straw, seeds, rain.
From so little, squash
takes off running,
honking her golden horn.

III. Talisman

Heirloom tomatoes still dream
of summer as I pick them, green
for jam. One drops to the ground
and I carry it for days in my pocket,
pull it out to sniff when I need
a shot of summer not yet gone.

IV. Walking, Dusk

Crows fly over,
inspecting the fields, return to light
in the muscled arms of the tree
perched at the edge of the ditch
where still a few apples hang
like cast off, rusty ornaments.

One stabs what's left of an apple,
flies off across the valley with four
in pursuit, weaving and diving
like stunt pilots as we watch,
cheering them on. Just when
we're all drunk on late season
apples, on fall's fleeting
light, the sun drops below
the ridge, and the crows
careen down the road,
slick black wings refracting
the last rays of light.

Farm Tour
The Day Before Equinox

Holly J. Hughes

We are here to glean what's left
of summer, sun sliding on across the fields,
up the long valley, its endless farewell.

Here, blueberry bushes hold summer
in green branches, nets flung over
to save them from crows who plot

in the firs. We walk down the hill,
plastic pail in hand, to pick
what's left, whatever remains.

At first, the berries hard to see,
but reaching into the heart
of the bush, we find each

quiet one on its thin stem. Then,
blueberry picking meditation:
not too fast or you'll knock them off,

just one small berry after the next,
hand moving from sky to earth,
bush to bucket, an arc that completes

summer, that will carry us
into fall. For now, we are alone
with each last second of summer,

picking each berry as if our lives depend
on it, holding it carefully, tenderly,
before dropping it into the bucket.

originally published in *Windfall*, 2011

The Woman In The Garden

Heather Hamilton

for R.R.

The woman in the garden has toes painted
the color of a sunset grown of rhododendrons.
She prances the paper callouses of her feet
against mulch, she presses close
and still while the moon sighs under the wings
of a hundred stone-grey owls. While the wind
crosses breath with shadow. While the ground
rests tilled and open. She is unexpected
and ordinary and safe. Or – imagine this –
she floats her nightgown across the open
faces of magnolias. She is flying.

The garden is sunbloomed. Awake. The woman
is sunbloomed. Awake. Her eyes are closed.
Her feet are crossed at the toes – painted the color
of a sunset grown of rhododendrons. Her hair
    floats
like the dander under the wings of a hundred
stone-grey owls. The moon sighs. The moon sighs.
The woman in the garden is awake.

She is flying, she is holding white poppies under
her eyelids, she is flying. Why there would be rocks
(shattered) why there would be darkness (split)
why there would be cracks (sewn) why
there would be a woman. Her eyes open, her eyes
spill. She is there. She is there. She is there.

The woman: the garden. She floats. She
lies – softly – on the ground, among turrets
of hyacinth that forgot to bloom, but now –
what else is there but the sweet, sweet, sweet.
The ground rests tilled and open. The moon sighs
under the wings of a hundred stone-grey owls.
The woman in the garden – the sweet, sweet,
sweet – all her hushed worn echo – all her bright
soft shimmer – the woman in her garden,
she is awake.

In The Orchard

Irene Bloom

When the heat of late summer blankets the island,
I steal out after dark,
like a thief looking to recapture the memories
of an earlier era.

Sometimes I go naked into the night
after the ozone proof panels
have been retracted and the hum
of atmospheric filters are silenced.

I slink around the agro domes
that glow like large luminous mushrooms,
hoping to remember the way
to the old orchard.

In a patch of darkness
I suddenly feel the bliss of a real breeze.
My body tingles in the dusty warm air mingled
with the pollen of a few rogue weeds.

Tonight, the path lies ahead
brightened by that steady satellite,
the one we could always rely on
to show us the way beneath the trees.

Slower now, I lumber towards
the very spot where we devoured your
peach and blackberry pie, exchanged so many
soft whispers and kisses full of promise.

There are still a few trees gnarled with age.
Rotten fruits cover the ground where
no wasps or birds garner their sweet remains.
They too are gone
All gone like you.

Desert, Sun, Water

Christine Walsh Rogers

You are angry, yet beautiful
Like a woman possessed
At first glance, gray and bare
Devoid of all life
Then the glimpses of color
Begin to caress my eyes
Red, like the blood you have
Drained, stains your walls
Shades of green and yellow
Touch down in the caverns
and crooks, where water once
Roared over you
You are not barren but bountiful
Wild bursts of pink and purple
Scattered throughout the brown dust
At one moment, still and quiet
The next, winds swirl in a thousand
Directions at once, warning
Visitors of your power and fury
You are to be revered, respected
Even feared
Relentlessly caressing me, while
Breathing new days into you
The sun unleashes all she has

To offer and you reach for her
Open wide and wide open
Water, blue as the cloudless sky
Above you, defies nature
Cool and still, it invites
Calls for me to ripple its surface
It is your mirror, where you survey your beauty and
Revel in your unique glory
Lulling me into a false sense of security
As the blue sky turns black
Filling with impossibly near moons
And ages dark stars
The scorching heat of your days
Becomes the ripping cold of your nights
I am humbled by all that you are

wonderwoman

afrose fatima ahmed

    every woman is a wonder
wrapped in flesh awe inspired
    by the blush of skin
under a fierce sun our bodies working
    to bring life out of the earth
& ether whether birth or
    plant or the alchemy of
magic that makes us witches
    a woman is reason & reinvention
all wrapped up
    in a reckoning

an ode to wednesday market

afrose fatima ahmed

all bus lines lead here
    this small square
where the air is infused with
    lion's mane and green leaf
both living & harvested
    the peony in the middle
of the week, more restful weekend
    than satuday's thrum,
even the ground we walk on
    given over to
imagination.

an ode to
the saturday market

afrose fatima ahmed

   the harvests
or every other day are poured
     into the basket of
saturday. at the market, i am
     here to see & be seen
by blueberry, begonia, & wayward
     bumblebee. the street sprouting
tents & becoming busy alleys
     where mystery is brewed
along with coffee, & every pass
     along every vendor reveals
new beauty.

Another Ode To Autumn

Carol Light

Blueberry. Blackberry.
We are bush and bramble gleaners.
We swat winged pests
with our stained fingers.

A blue barrow tips
beside a row of rusting blooms.
Seed heavy heads droop yellow–
petals into furrows swoon.

We peer through pane-free windows,
orchard door open to gust and sky;
Limbs lace red and russet beads–
Bramley. Pippin. Northern Spy.

Fenced among the apple boughs,
they nudge and huddle, these unshorn sheep.
Does a flock dream of pomace?
Geese in feathered meadows sleep.

Salmon shy and nearly dry
this time of year, grass chokes the creek.
Now the thistledown is brown,
and the yellow jackets leak,

    stalking sweet all afternoon, and autumn peals a
        bronze bell.
Now violet murmurs stun the sky
where dusky starlings turn and swell.

Wording The Land
Guest Poets

AFROSE FATIMA AHMED is a hybrid Texan-Washingtonian who writes poems on emerald city streets and at the tops of evergreen trees. She is the daughter of Muslim immigrants from India. Her body and her art live in liminal spaces: polar US borderlands, the division between land and sea, the place where urban density drops off into rural solitude. Afrose comes to poetry as just one avenue for creating experiences of beauty and communion for herself and other people. Her writing emphasizes all the senses and acknowledges a world in which humans are suffering and experiencing bliss against wild landscapes that are simultaneously living and dying.

GARY COPELAND LILLEY is a native of Sandy Cross, North Carolina. He is a veteran of the United States Navy Submarine Force and a longtime blues denizen of Washington, DC and Chicago. He presently teaches and writes in Port Townsend, Washington. Lilley's books include *Alpha Zulu*, *The Subsequent Blues*, *Black Poem* and *The Reprehensibles*.

CAROL LIGHT'S poetry has appeared in *Narrative Magazine*, *Poetry Northwest*, *32 Poems*, *American Life in Poetry*, on the Poetry Foundation website, and elsewhere. Her book, *Heaven from Steam*, was published in 2014 by Able Muse Press. She has received awards from Artist Trust and Jack Straw Productions. She has taught writing at the University of Washington, the University of Iowa, Peninsula and Olympic Colleges, the Compass Rose Learning Collective, and the Port Townsend Public Schools. She lives with her family in Port Townsend.

MATTHEW NIENOW is the author of *House of Water* (Alice James Books, 2016), as well as several chapbooks, including *The End of the Folded Map* (Codhill Press, 2011). He has been recognized with Fellowships from *Poetry Magazine* and the Poetry Foundation, The National Endowment for the Arts, and Artist Trust. He lives in Port Townsend with his wife and two sons, where he teaches at Jefferson Community School and runs Good Story Paddle Boards.

Lunch With The Devil

Matthew Nienow

We have the coq au vin, a fricassee
of old rooster thickened with roux,
the older the bird, he says, *the richer
the sauce.* He plucks the bouquet garni
dripping with the sweet juice,
drops it on a small dish and licks
his fingers, which are delicate
instruments, plump, but agile,
calloused, but smooth. He raises
his Burgundy and when our glasses
meet, the sound could mean nothing
other than *eat*! *Do not be shy*
and so I am not shy and ask
how it felt to burn his paintings
just to keep warm, how his father's
face looked when he realized
his son had surpassed him,
but he only smiles and drinks
more wine, sucking at the bones
before dropping them back
in the stew, sopping up the sauce
with a crust of bread, his hands
working over the bowl with precision.

When the bill comes he flips it over
and reaches into his coat, saying,
let me, they will not take my money here—
I put up a little fuss for show,
but watch closely as he writes
the check, businesslike, and begins
sketching the maître d' on the back.
For ten minutes we sit in near silence
while the man appears on the page,
until he looks up and says, *tell me
this drawing isn't worth more than our lunch.*
I look away because I don't know
and wouldn't tell him if I did.

first appeared in *Devil's Lake*

Allergy Song

Matthew Nienow

Come and I will clear your throat of lilacs,
tease loose the knots of a blossom's work,
I'll make a tonic stronger than the pollen
that put you here, propped up at the edge
of the bed, a nectarine shirt tossed over
the lampshade making the whole room glow
orange, as I imagine it might inside a flower,
as if we were bees, you with your book
of hunger, me with my song of hum and pause—

For you I'll sleep with windows closed
even though the sweet air swims against the glass,
and the cedar whispers the story of before us
and the night bird sings your name, *sweet, sweet,
    sweet*—

wife, before I knew you I slept outside
for months at a time and gathered a store of
    things:

blue fishing twine, a glass jar the color of sky,
a rusted knife handle missing its blade, caribou
    antler,
bone carvings, a small stone cairn—
and deep in the pages of a tattered journal,
two sprigs of River Beauty,
the blossom's purple faded slightly, but still
    fragrant,
a gift, because I love you, I will not share.

first appeared in *Prairie Schooner*

Spring Planting

Matthew Nienow

I told a friend how I had tilled
my fiancé's garden,
laying my shirt over the post
of the fence, working in the May noon,
the susurration of brief rain
on my shoulders,
on the shoulders of earth turning,
the hoe entering soil as a hand,
searching the damp places,
offering light to what was
previously intimate with the dark.

For me, it was only a favor
related to vegetables,
but the friend, shifting in her seat,
cheeks warming with blood,
only wanted to see my hands
dirt lathered, worn, as if expecting
a field to unfold.

first appeared in *Poet Lore*

Finnriver Pantoum

Roseanna Almaee-Nejadi

The land anchors my soul
It brings me to tears, makes me whole
The light, the air pulls me down
To sink my toes into the ground

It brings me to tears, makes me whole
This Finnriver, S'Klallam land so old
To sink my toes into the ground
Make whole my grief, heal the wound

The valley, the bounty fed all around
The light, the air pulls me down
All who come are made whole
This land anchors the soul.

Wording The Land

Roseanna Almaee-Nejadi

Fingertips brush tops of flowers, grasses
And scents fill the air as sun warms the earth
The soul, body aches with joy or grief
Stretches, lies prostrate
As The Mother opens, welcomes and heals.

Pour it in, let all joy and grief flow forth.
The Mother responds, whispers through bough
    and bird song.
Let go; pour your words into the land
For absolution, for healing.

We word the land with our joys and sorrows, and
The Mother takes it all, gives back more.

Untitled

Roxane Hudson

The land beneath my feet
Swells and teems with life
Smaller than my eye
A universe of life & death & rebirth
supporting us all.

Untitled

Diane Morency

Spring
Tender green shoots push thru newly warmed earth
Pea tendrils curl upwards
Rain bathes the garden
Pregnant with promise.

> Gray cat
> Scouting out catnip pot
> Surprised fat bee

Summer
Bursting out of its bed
Yellow squash fight with tomatoes
Fragrant thyme and basil hold back
Unruly oregano
I pop a warm blueberry into my mouth
Face in the sun.

> Gray cat
> Bows to the sun
> Masterful yogi

Fall
Full moon lights the fall garden
Last of summer's bounty harvested
A chill wind
I sit wrapped in a blanket
Breathing the earth

> Gray cat
> Curled into the moon light
> Watches garden gate

Winter
Garden rest under a blanket of snow
Gone the bees
Silent the peep frogs
Seed catalogs
I leave the garden sleeping Plan for our joyful
Spring awakening.

> Gray cat
> Silent garden Budd
> Mantle of snow

Hooray, Hooray, It's Market Day

Judy Drechsler

Peaked white roofs point towards the rising sun.
Market day in Port Townsend! I walk up
    the street,
basket swinging from my hand.
The buzz of small town conversations reach
    me first,
the music of guitar and keyboard bounce into
    my ears.

Vendor carts filled with beauty from local
    organic farms
line both sides of the street, march down
    the middle.
A riotous disarray, smells of baking bread,
    grilled salmon,
bratwurst. A delicate lust makes me
buy more than I can possibly eat.

Cheeses, tasty award winners, sit on
    crispy crackers.
Purple Lilacs, red and yellow Dahlias, frilled
    pink tulips,
soy candles with appealing names, Eggplant,
    Heirloom
Tomato, Cinderella Pumpkin, Lemon Basil, all
eager to light the way to my evening dinner table.

Golden, deep green, and brilliant orange squash of
    all shapes
spill out from baskets and boxes.
Beans abound, purple, yellow, white and green,
lay in untidy heaps,
flanked by crisp green and white striped zucchini
    and juicy
tomatoes in an array of yellows and reds.

They fill my swinging basket to overflowing.
In my mind I see them sitting on my kitchen
    counter,
as much at home in the stillness of my kitchen as
    at the busy market.
My dinner plate waits patiently for their goodness.

Farm Tour Perfume

Lynn Fritsche

Warm sun on my head and a
Cool breeze in my face.
Sweet, musky base notes with
Grassy, green top notes.
A heart note of contentment.

Farm perfume marries up the
Scents of new friends
Two-footed, four-footed,
Hairy and hoofed,
Woolly, winged,
Feathered and furred,
A few well-scented humans, too!

Five Haiku

Oma Landstra

Whirlwinds of beautiful leaves fly
Into autumn's clear air
Sunshine and transformation await.

Furrows of rich soil
Put to bed for a rest
Promise of seedlings.

My garden, so beautiful
Pumpkins lively and bright
Consider their future.

Gay children skip
Into rows of pumpkins
Merrily carrying theirs home.

Cool winds swirl
Leaves dance playfully
Fall is a celebration.

Spring Equinox

For Judith Kitchen

Shelia Bender

I've washed a winter's worth of collard greens,
torn the leaf from stems and veins, steamed
the greens in broth, adding red pepper flakes,
cayenne, too, then ate the fans I'd frayed
and mixed with rice and beans.
I triple washed the beets, separating greens
from bulbous roots. Steamed and boiled,
they helped me pull away from winter,
start remembering it's spring.

The peas go in, the onion sets, more fava beans,
soon cauliflower and tomatoes, the orange,
yellow, green, and maybe striped as well.
I plucked last year's shriveled figs, born too late
to ripen on our maturing tree, tossed them behind
our fence with prayers that figs might sweeten
sooner now that years are moving faster toward
     an end
that I refuse to really see, though I know how fast
the growing and faster still we eat.

Untitled

Pierce Kennedy

Bishops and the sacred cow,
in black and white,
milk-precious, without
purchase and low and dry.

The naked creek, grass choked and
settled straight,
glaring tepid
and still.

Pastures billow to seed, to
meter winter inches dropped
in ridge and rain.

Then tender hands, unglinting
and radicle, fit stock and whip,
with a careful bevel and tendril intent.

Then hands, roughed, craft
the creek's myth, cool, leaved,
and rippling.

The geese neat canary
yields to limbs adorned,
to sun-sweet shades, to rustling
leaves and lips.
These ornaments aflame,
black seeded and heaving,
run clear and spirited.

BZZZZZ

Richard Coletta

Today I went to mow the lawn and realized I was not alone.
Amid the dandelions and grass, every time I made a pass
trying to de-weed my yard, I realized I had to guard against my mower
running over something hiding in the clover . . . something I could barely see,
no bigger than a goober pea—a tiny little bumble bee.
He just kept looking up at me—following me all around, wandering up and down there
close to the ground, making that sound.
His buzzing had a certain tone—"Leave my dandelions alone" he seemed to shout,
as close as I could figure out.

It seems these last ten years or so, for reasons I don't really know,
I've stopped just swatting bees (and spiders).
I must admit that I've provided spider rides— that's how I guided them outside,
in little jars to my back yard to set them free. It just makes perfect sense to me.

Perhaps it is a little Zen of me, to be considerate
　　of a bee, but not to be seems just so wrong.
It never really takes that long to help them in their
　　small requests.
How're you supposed to treat your guests?

Well, to get back to my new mown lawn . . . I have
　　to say, it does look wrong.
In trying to appease the bees, I may have taken
　　liberties.
My lawn may look like a jigsaw puzzle . . .
but I'm glad it's filled with bumble bee buzzle.

　　originally published in *Special Pants*

Walk Straight

Kia Armstrong

A July sun rises, and like countless dawns before
their time this crew is off and racing
to beat the heat.

An intimate understanding of what must be done
today tomorrow
forever
is a tool for survival,
methodically wielded like well-honed knives.

Does the spinach scream with each slice of the
    blade?
Does it protest being bunched and banded?
Did it learn to suffer in silence long ago?
Who is trained
to hear its cries?

Shadows rise and fall as bodies crouch and bend.
White sun bears strong,
brown eyes cast down to earth
up to God.

Proud, tired feet
walk straight
down field rows
and everywhere they go.

Feeding The Goats At Sunfield

Alex C. Eisenberg

He held four bottles of fresh
sloshing milk
two in each enormous hand.
I stood holding
nothing & reached too late
to offer help.

He thrust both his fists
like swollen udders
through an opening
between electricity & iron
so every teat could meet
a single suckling snout.

Helplessly
I watched
his broad body brace
against the push-pull frenzy of the kids
–their eager lips
their wild flapping ears
their rectangle alien eyes.

His hands tensed
gripping four bottles
tight between fat fingers
dripping like nipples
strained & strange.
I only watched: this need;
this love; this man
become mother.

Fall Fog Has Settled Again Over Discovery Bay

Sheila Bender

Wrapped in the low cloud, I wish for summer
and clear skies, an early morning
stroll through the garden ripe with peas,
raspberries, remembered laughter
of my visiting grandsons who order "pancakes
as big as the plate" during their visits.

A therapist said, "Wish is a child's word,"
so I go out into the chilly, damp air. A cucumber
hides beneath large leaves, a patty pan squash
might yet ripen. Amidst the curves of
     the vegetables,
I see again my grandsons' feet in brand
     new Crocs.

One morning the older boy packed the tomatoes
he picked to take home. His younger brother
sprayed a blue chalk face on our garden gate.
The next day the older one ate the ripened
     strawberries;
the younger one lay still in bed watching
our cat who slept at his feet.

At the raised beds, I recollect the boys' tan bodies
as they ran around stacked cottage stones
     pulling kale
leaves to mark each lap. If wish is a child's word,
I raise my coffee cup in toast to memories
I love, still fresh and young.

Curves and Angles

Leticia Huber

Curves and angles
Flowing freely
On the edges
Of a leaf of
A lettuce

I admiringly see them
Dancing
A light and dark green dance
Of chlorophyll
And iron
And water
And calcium
And sodium
And magnesium
And potassium
And protein
And vitamins
And fiber
And sun

At the same time
All of them
Dancing the dance of life
All of them
And earth
At the same time
No mistakes
Total harmony
In the curves and angles
Flowing freely
On the edges

Of a leaf of
Lettuce

The leaf
On my salad
The leaf
On my sandwich
Enticing my eyes
To bring my body
Into hunger
For all that
Fresh beauty
That promises
Sweetness
Freshness
Nutrition
And fun
To my mouth
That opens
Delightedly
Unavoidably
To make
Such freshness
Mine

Make it part of me
Literally
Since its components
Will enter my blood
And become
My body
Itself
In just
A few minutes
From
The second
I consume

It
And deep in my cells
I will feel nurtured

By these leaves
So sweet
So quenching
Such a product of the earth

Earth
Opened patiently
By loving hands
Earth
Opened respectfully
By caring hearts
Earth
Made pregnant
With seeds
And amazement
With sun
Air
And water
By the farmer's hand

Made pregnant
With care
With knowledge
With sweat
With curiosity
With dreams
By the farmer's hand

That hand
Like mine

That hand
Seeding and growing

From the earth itself
Those plants
That feed me
Those plants
That
Entering my body
Build the tissues of my body
One by one

The hands of the farmers
Who help my body
Build its hands
With the food I eat
With the food farmers grow
From the earth

Miracle accomplished!

Miracle to feed each generation
Of me
And you
Through millennia
From the earth

Through the earth

As it always
Has been

Brightness

Liz Crain

The awakening, first sprout of seed through soil, opening; the confirmation of life. This is a beautiful place! We are almost there, your thoughts have finally swam into my dreams and together, there is infinite understanding between gazing hearts. Through eternal embezzlement of emotion, one cannot reach center balance and attain true enlightenment. Through external joy and the giving of all our secrets to the sun, light will shine within and the explosive force of truth radiates from our new found core. These lessons find us in the dark, pull at our heart strings for better or worse, rake the sludge of past failure off our backs, and present us to ourselves anew. Rebirth happens again and again, with confidence, walk out of this cave of perpetual blindness and awaken. No flower hides from the sun.

St. Helens

Peter G. Quinn

A grape stained piece of canvas
held bread, apples, cheese
an anonymous bottle of wine
theifed from a barrel, tagged
with brix sugar, crush date.

We worked Yamhill vineyards
pulled weeds, liberated, trained
vines, absorbed the metre,
measure of – outside, felt gentle
pulse of a volcano as it sighed in, out
purging what was too much for it

to hold.

We watched the volcano channel,
sixty miles away, it filled the screen.
We sat on the tailgate in red
Dundee hills drank in life as St. Helens
built to deadly, silent then,
uncaring of our point in its time.

Chimacum Jr. Sr. High School Garden

Margaret Garrett

I am greeted by the scent of lavender as I enter the
 garden gate.
Blueberry plants are fall-green, gone are the
 berries eaten with joy in the warm sunshine.

Dahlias boast the rich colors of fall on strong
 stocks, enjoying the days coolness.

Tomatoes still ripen on 8-foot vines in the cozy-
 warm green house.
Basil planted by the tall plant's feet await a date
 with olive oil, fresh mozzarella and the last of
 those beautiful tomatoes.
Onions are ready to be chopped by the culinary
 arts class and cooked
with the fresh-dug potatoes that horticulture class
 grew.
Dark green kale stands tall having survived the
 summer heat: kale whose taste and texture
 add depth to stew and soup on a cold winter
 day.

Multi-color corn hangs from the rafters drying.
Compost has been spread along the garden rows
 to feed the ground over the long rainy days
 ahead.

I will be roasting the rich root vegetables of the fall
 garden as I dream of that first bite of a
 sun-warm tomato.

A Farmer's Poem

Halcyon Stoker-Graham, 13

Nothing to me is quite as grounding
as the feeling of earth in my hands.
My trade is an old one.
I've known this land for years, just
like the people before me knew it,
and just like the generation that lived before them.

These bonds are deep.
These nights are quiet.
Summer is folding gently into autumn;
it will be harvest time here soon.

The moon thins through the cold damp evenings
while leaves and apples fall.
The goats are asleep between warm bales; the
chickens dream from their roosts.

When morning comes it will be just as
extraordinary as the last,
if not more. For when then sun dawns
I know it is time to till the patches,
to let the hens range freely in the field,
to check in on the goats and sheep,
to share the profits of fruit and root
with the world that leans on us.

Seasons in the Orchard

Crystie Kisler

March

It's turning time
time for our latitude to lean into the light
time for buds to swell
time for mud to melt
time for roots to relax
time for pruning, for weeding, for wondering
when the first blossom will break free

June

June, your heat is here too soon!
Where is your summer shower
making earth a greener bower?
This warmth is making me swoon!

July

These deep days of summer stretch time
with lingering light long into the night
each moment a marathon
running to keep up with itself.

September

And here they come!
Ripe, ready, round, red,
green, golden, globes,
sweet, sour, sharp,
fine, firm, fleshy fruit

The apples are here! The apples are here!

October Apples

Plucked, picked, pulled from the branch
Tucked, tossed, packed into the bag
Piled, dropped, dumped into the bin
Delivered, funneled, fed into the press
Pumped, pressured, poured into the tank
Sipped, swallowed, savored, from the glass!

Winter Wheat

Abby Jorgensen

First the grain is buried under dark earth,
early in the fall, the way that all things
able to understand light must first
be buried. Damp seed cracks open

after the ordeal and shoots of green appear
well before this glacial valley remembers much
about green – the shadowy jade of fir
and cedar boughs, notwithstanding.

When it reaches a height most glorious,
able to be blown by gusty winds into galactic
    patterns
reflective of our milky way, just past the peak
of its vascular incarnation, a diesel combine
    arrives

to harvest golden stalks and again, these small
    miracles
go dormant – dried, milled, bagged – and they
    wait.
Do they exist with a consciousness of potential
not yet realized? A jar arrives at my door,
    delivered

by the farmer's son, and I breathe it in – a malty,
nutty smell. Time to build the levain with a well-
	seasoned
starter from an old friend. Over the next
twenty four hours it will be mixed, folded,

slapped, stretched,
punched, and kneaded
until finally, this grain, which has now lain
in wait at least a half dozen times, has already

given sustenance to birds and mice and a
	thousand
smaller beings, delivers to our bodies the patience
of saints and the nutrients of a land made rich
by the bones of mastodon and salmon.

Muffin Therapy

Irene Bloom

This morning the light barely seeps
into my room through a thick winter fog.
The bed, a heap of tangled sheets,
reminds me of the struggles of sleep.

But soon, the sky becomes clear.
Anxiety fades away
as an image of muffins
brightens my clouded brain.

Today I'll need no doctor's couch,
no pills to calm the nerves,
for baking is the remedy
after another worrisome night.

Tools for healing are in a kitchen drawer-
measuring cup and spatula,
a silver nest of spoons
to portion soda and cinnamon.

The soothing motions commence,
placing crisp paper liners
into a dozen perfect holders-
one for each mound of cake.

And now the familiar mixing
of dry into wet,
flour and oats
into milk and eggs.

Folding and stirring
the flavors combine.
The oven is hot, the house
smells of warm sugar.

The first bite is crunchy and moist.
A taste of nut and date,
a mug of steamy tea,
and all is well in the world.
.

Souvlaki

Irene Bloom

The steam train stopped
At a place I could not pronounce
But I didn't care
Hunger speaks a common language
And as I hung out the window
They were there
Alongside the car
Shouting and reaching up
with their wares
and I squinting through the steam
swallowing the foreign sounds and smells
heard Souvlaki
And signaled for two
Fatty and spiced
I wish I had eaten more
As the train belched forward
I caught a glimpse of
So many sticks strewn on the platform

In Ghent

Irene Bloom

where every Medieval street
holds a myriad of wonders
where the massive Castle of the Counts
still stands in the city center

where atop a belfy tower
a gilded dragon still guards the town
and the giant god Neptune
adorns the old fish market gate

I can only conjur up my breakfast
at the inn on Vlaanderenstraat
It's not the taste of smooth Belgian ale
in an outdoor café

nor the smell of butter cream truffles
in the corner chocolatier
but the beauty of a simple boiled egg
not too hard or runny soft

perfect in its white porcelain cup
alongside a fresh croissant
a plate of cheese and a carafe
of freshly brewed coffee

at the small square table
with its white starched cloth
napkin in my lap
in the tiny sunlit room

where we sat
my daughter and I
chatting about our day
in this place the gem of Flanders

About the Publisher

Marcia Breece/Publishing Partners offers innovative, flexible, and affordable alternatives for independent authors. An à la carte menu includes editing, cover design, interior design/layout, printing, ebook layout, and distribution.

Authors retain ownership and control of their content, collect 100% of royalties and successfully compete with major publishing houses through print, eBooks or audiobooks.

The goal is clear: as your publishing partner, she will help you produce a book you can be proud of. She offers the high quality, affordable services you'll need to have the best possible self-publishing experience.

marcia@marciabreece.com
www.marciabreece.com

www.ingramcontent.com/pod-product-compliance
Lightning Source LLC
Chambersburg PA
CBHW020129130526
44591CB00032B/578